PARANORMAL LIFE CYCLES

VAMPIRE

By
Noah Leatherland

All rights reserved.
Printed in India.

A catalogue record for this
book is available
from the British Library.

ISBN 978-1-80505-681-2

Written by
Noah Leatherland

Edited by
Robin Twiddy

Designed by
Drue Rintoul

©2024
BookLife Publishing Ltd.
King's Lynn, Norfolk
PE30 4LS, UK

All facts, statistics, web addresses and URLs in this book were verified as valid and accurate at time of writing.
No responsibility for any changes to external websites or references can be accepted by either the author or publisher.

AN INTRODUCTION TO BOOKLIFE RAPID READERS...

Packed full of gripping topics and twisted tales, BookLife Rapid Readers are perfect for older children looking to propel their reading up to top speed. With three levels based on our planet's fastest animals, children will be able to find the perfect point from which to accelerate their reading journey. From the spooky to the silly, these roaring reads will turn every child at every reading level into a prolific page-turner!

CHEETAH

The fastest animals on land, cheetahs will be taking their first strides as they race to top speed.

MARLIN

The fastest animals under water, marlins will be blasting through their journey.

FALCON

The fastest animals in the air, falcons will be flying at top speed as they tear through the skies.

IMAGE CREDITS

All images courtesy of Shutterstock.com. With thanks to Getty Images, Thinkstock Photo and iStockphoto. Cover – KingJC, Sergio Photone, Here, Jakub Krechowicz, sociologas, wabeno. Recurring – Elizaveta Mironets, sociologas, wabeno. P1 – KingJC. P4–5 – madorf, Raggedstone. P6–7 – LedyX, Ysbrand Cosijn. P8–9 – Carlos Caetano, Margaret M Stewart. P10–11 – marinafrost, Rawpixel.com. P12–13 – FOTOKITA, Kiselev Andrey Valerevich. P14–15 – Kiselev Andrey Valerevich, Subbotina Anna. P16–17 – Fer Gregory, Sola Solandra. P18–19 – iobard, Warpaint. P20–21 – DarkBird, Stone36. P22–23 – Fer Gregory, Selin Serhii. P24–25 – Dm_Cherry, LightField Studios, patrickdifeliciantonio, Plus69. P26–27 – A_Lesik, Marian Weyo, Melinda Nagy. P28–29 – freya-photographer, serpeblu. P30 – mRGB.

CONTENTS

PAGE 4	What Is a Life Cycle?
PAGE 6	What Is a Vampire?
PAGE 8	The Curse Begins
PAGE 10	The Early Vampire
PAGE 12	The Fully Transformed Vampire
PAGE 14	Diet
PAGE 16	Habitat
PAGE 18	The Old Vampire
PAGE 20	Passing on the Curse
PAGE 22	Types of Vampire
PAGE 24	Spotting a Vampire
PAGE 26	How to Deal with a Vampire
PAGE 28	Life Cycle of a Vampire
PAGE 30	Beware the Paranormal!
PAGE 31	Glossary
PAGE 32	Index

Words that look like this can be found in the glossary on page 31.

WHAT IS A LIFE CYCLE?

All living things have a life cycle. Across their life cycle, living things grow and change. They might only change a little bit with each step of the life cycle, or they might change a lot.

Living things <u>reproduce</u> so the life cycle can keep going. It is normal for living things to die as part of the life cycle.

But not everything in this world is normal. Some creatures are so strange that they can only be called paranormal.

Some paranormal creatures start their life cycles as normal living things. Then, something happens to them. Something... evil.

That is exactly how the blood-soaked life cycle of the vampire begins...

WHAT IS A VAMPIRE?

Vampires are very mysterious creatures. Stories about vampires have been found all over the world. Some of these stories are thousands of years old.

Vampires are not quite dead, but they are not quite alive either. They are somewhere in between the two.

There is one thing that is certain about vampires. They want to suck your blood!

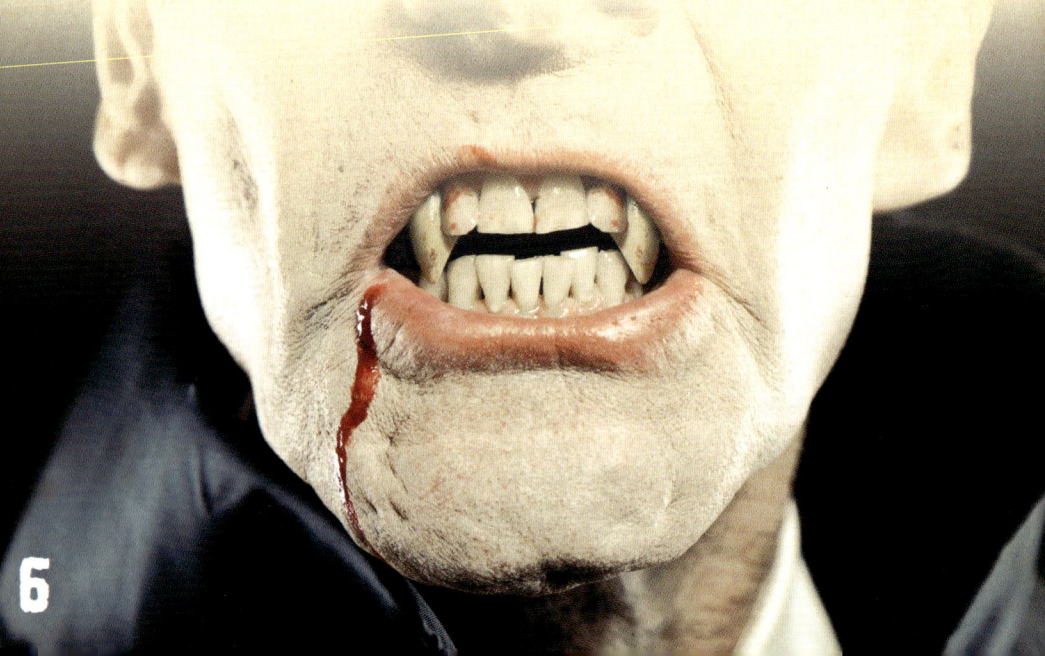

No one knows where they came from. No one knows how many vampires there are in the world, either. But vampires have a life cycle just like every other creature in the world. Learning their life cycle can help you stay safe.

Be warned. Vampires are very good at hiding. There could be a vampire near you right now...

THE CURSE BEGINS

Nobody is safe from the vampire's curse. Most people do not even realise they have been cursed until it is too late. The curse begins with a vampire's bite.

It is a terrifying moment. A chill down the spine. A rush of terror. Then, two sharp fangs digging into skin!

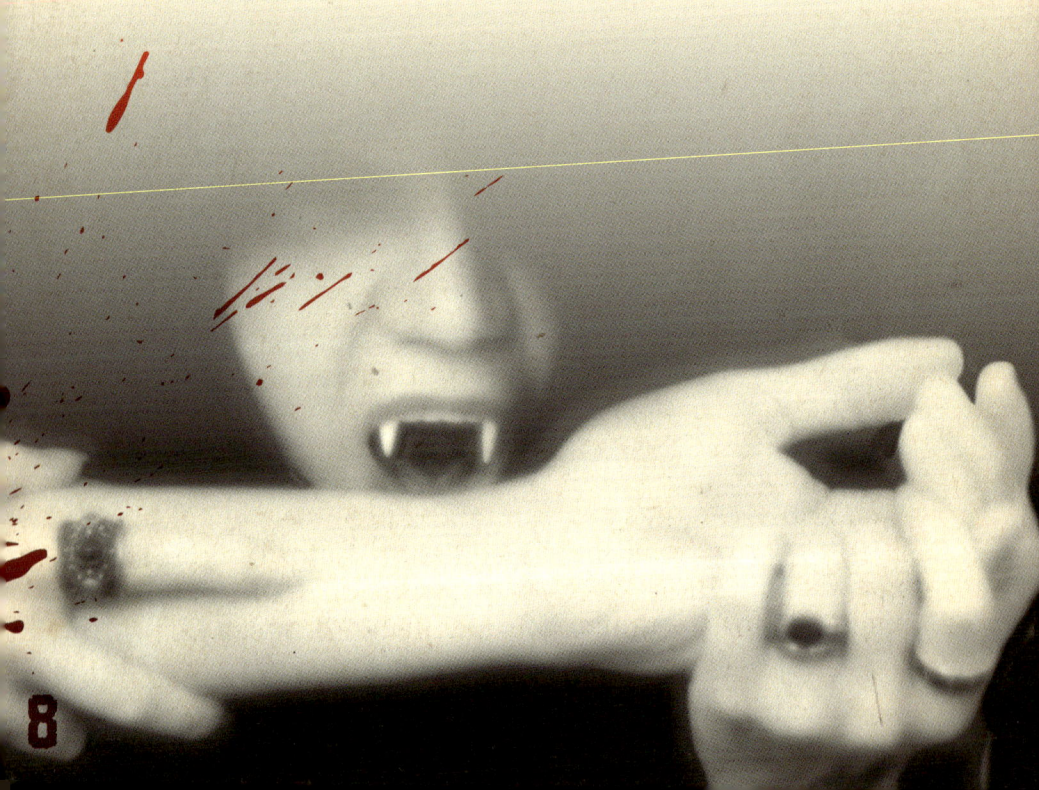

If the vampire decides to let them live, the person they have bitten becomes cursed. When they wake up, they may not remember what happened to them.

But there is one way they can tell that they have been cursed. There will be two small spots where the vampire bit them.

Soon, they will start to feel the curse...

THE EARLY VAMPIRE

A person does not become a vampire straight away. It takes time for the curse to <u>transform</u> them.

First, they will feel the curse taking over their body... and it does not feel nice. They will start to sweat and shake. Their skin may start turning pale.

People might think the curse is just an illness. They are very wrong...

Next, the soon-to-be vampire will feel a sharp pain in their mouth.

Humans have pointy teeth called canines. When a human becomes a vampire, their top two canine teeth change. They become longer and sharper. It hurts a lot when they grow like this. They become the pointy fangs of a vampire!

THE FULLY TRANSFORMED VAMPIRE

Once they have grown their pointy fangs, the transformation is complete. The cursed person is now a vampire.

The vampire stays at this stage in its life cycle for hundreds of years. Vampires do not age much at all. Years later, they may look the same as they did on the day they were bitten.

The curse also gives the vampires some special powers. Vampires can transform into bats and fly through the night. Transforming into a bat helps them stay hidden in the darkness.

Vampires are also able to <u>hypnotise</u> people. When vampires hypnotise someone, they can make them do anything they want. This can lead to some deadly things...

DIET

There is one thing that makes up the vampire's diet. Blood! Lots and lots of blood.

The vampire's curse makes them <u>crave</u> blood. Their thirst for blood can become very painful. The longer a vampire goes without blood, the more <u>aggressive</u> they become. This means that the most dangerous kind of vampire is a thirsty vampire.

Some types of blood taste much sweeter on a vampire's tongue than others. The blood of a kind, <u>innocent</u> human is the sweetest.

Vampires use their fangs to bite two holes into a person's neck. Then, they suck the blood out with their mouths. A vampire can drink all the blood in a person's body in a few minutes!

HABITAT

A vampire's skin burns when they are in sunlight. So, vampires need to live in the shadows.

Many vampires can be found living in castles. Castles are very dark inside and keep vampires safe from any angry humans that try to hunt them.

Castles also have lots of room for vampires to hide their secrets...

Vampires sleep best in total darkness. So, a lot of vampires like to sleep inside coffins that keep the light out. Some vampires even sleep in coffins made of stone to be extra careful.

Vampires like to live near humans. This means they don't have to go far to find fresh blood.

THE OLD VAMPIRE

After living for hundreds of years, the vampire finally reaches the final stage of its life cycle. Over the years, the vampire starts to look less and less like a human and more like a bat.

All their hair falls out. Their ears become pointy and the rest of their teeth become as sharp as their fangs.

The vampire's curse grows stronger over their life. When the vampire reaches the final part of their life cycle, they are at their most powerful.

A few vampires even get new powers as they get older. Some can move objects with their mind. Some can fly without needing to change into a bat!

PASSING ON
THE CURSE

Vampires are very sneaky hunters. However, sometimes they do not drink all the blood in a person's body. Instead, they bite and drink just enough to pass on the vampire's curse.

Vampires use lots of tricks to pass the curse on. They might try to make themselves look human and become friends with their <u>victim</u> first.

One night, the vampire invites the victim to their castle. While they are distracted, the vampire looks for a juicy spot on the victim's neck to sink their fangs into.

Even if the victim tries to run away, it is easy to get lost in a dark castle. You never know what is around the corner...

TYPES OF VAMPIRE

There are a few different kinds of vampires in the world.

PSYCHIC VAMPIRES

Some vampires do not crave blood. Instead, they are hungry for another part of a person... their mind!

Psychic vampires do not need to bite you. They just need to get close enough to use their powers to drain your brain.

REVENANTS

Revenants are a type of underlined undead vampire made by evil magic. Revenants drink blood, but it is not the only thing they want.

Revenants want <u>revenge</u>. They climb out of their graves to hunt down people who upset them during their lives. If they have to hunt for a long time, they will drink someone's blood to keep themselves going.

SPOTTING A VAMPIRE

Vampires can look a lot like humans. However, there are some things to watch out for to help you spot a vampire.

EYES

If you think someone is a vampire, watch their eyes. If they are looking at your neck, they could be planning their next bite!

AVOIDS SUNLIGHT

Vampires hate sunlight. Keep an eye on anyone staying in the dark...

MIRRORS

Vampires do not have a <u>reflection</u>. This means that when they look in a mirror, there is nothing there. If you think someone wants to suck your blood, check to see if they have a reflection.

RED DRINKS

Watch out for anyone taking a sip of something red. Who knows what could be in their glass...

How to Deal with a Vampire

If you find a vampire, do not panic! There are ways to protect yourself.

Garlic

Vampires hate the taste and smell of garlic. To make sure they do not bite you, rub some on yourself or keep some in your pockets.

Unwelcome Guests

Vampires cannot enter someone's house unless they are invited inside. Do not let them trick you!

LIGHT

Remember, sunlight burns a vampire's skin. Keep the curtains open. Stay in bright places during the day to make sure vampires stay away.

ROSES

Some stories say that wild roses can keep vampires away. Grow some in your garden to make sure vampires keep their distance.

You can always ask a vampire hunter for help!

LIFE CYCLE OF A VAMPIRE

It all starts with one bite. The unlucky ones have all their blood sucked out. The less unlucky ones end up cursed.

The curse transforms them into a vampire. Their teeth grow into deadly fangs, and they become thirsty for blood.

Fully transformed vampires look just like humans and use their powers to hunt down their victims.

Vampires start to look uglier as they get older. Their faces change to look even more like terrifying monsters. As they get older, they also get more powerful.

A vampire might give the curse to a few people in their life. No one really knows how long a vampire lives for. They might live for thousands of years!

Beware the Paranormal!

Vampires are not the only paranormal creatures in the world. There are plenty more horrific creatures hiding in the shadows. Some of them have to be seen to be believed.

But, as interesting as paranormal creatures are, make sure to stay away from them. Read and learn more about them, but do not go chasing after them!

GLOSSARY

AGGRESSIVE likely to attack

CRAVE to really want something

HYPNOTISE to make someone easily follow orders without being able to stop

INNOCENT someone who has not done anything wrong

REFLECTION an image made when light bounces off something

REPRODUCE to make more of the same thing

REVENGE when someone hurts another person for something they have done to them

PARANORMAL something that cannot be explained by science

TRANSFORM to turn into something else

UNDEAD dead but still able to move around

VICTIM someone who has something bad done to them

INDEX

BATS 13, 18–19

BLOOD 5–6, 14–15, 17, 20, 22–23, 25, 28

CASTLES 16, 21

COFFINS 17

FANGS 8, 11–12, 15, 18, 21, 28

GARLIC 26

MAGIC 23

MIRRORS 25

ROSES 27